My Mass Book

Sadlier
A Division of
William H. Sadlier Inc.
New York
Chicago
Los Angeles

Nihil Obstat
Reverend Benedict Ehmann
Censor Deputatus

Imprimatur
✠ Matthew H. Clark, D.D.
Bishop of Rochester
October 18, 1984

The nihil obstat and imprimatur are official declarations that a book or pamphlet is free of doctrinal or moral error. No implication is contained therein that those who have granted the nihil obstat and imprimatur agree with the contents, opinions or statements expressed.

Excerpts from the English translation of *The Roman Missal* © 1973, International Committee on English in the Liturgy, Inc. (ICEL). All rights reserved.

Copyright © 1985 by William H. Sadlier, Inc. All rights reserved. This book, or any part thereof, may not be reproduced in any form, or by any photographic, or mechanical, or by any sound recording system, or by any device for storage and retrieval of information, without the written permission of the publisher. Printed in the United States of America.

Home Office: 11 Park Place, New York, NY 10007.

ISBN 0-8215-2374-0
3456789/9876

Designer: Creative Group, Inc.
Art Director: Julius Bronstein
Illustrations: Robert Gleason
Cover photo: Wes Thomas

Ask someone in your family to help you fill in your Baptismal Card.

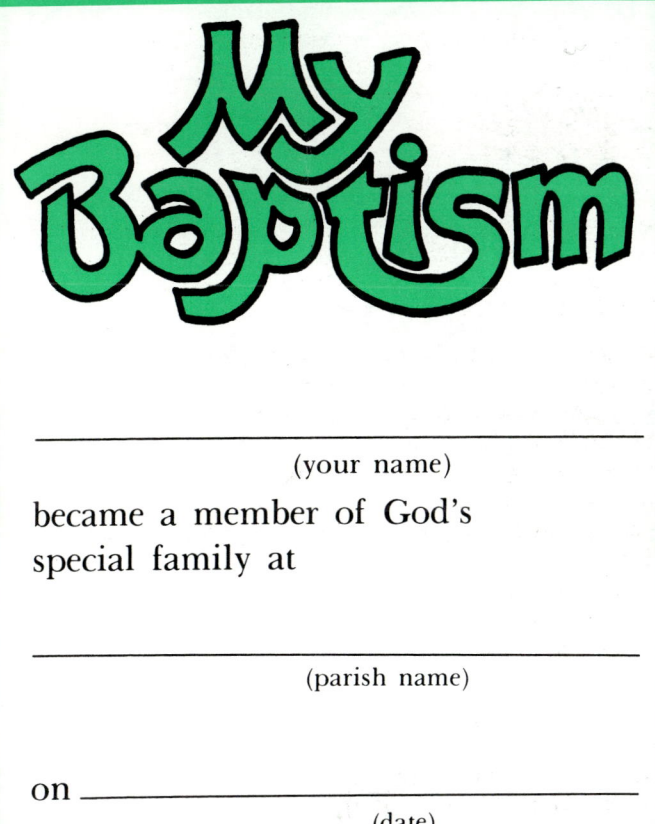

My Baptism

_____
(your name)

became a member of God's special family at

_____
(parish name)

on _____
(date)

The Mass begins with the gathering and welcoming of God's family.

Decorate the welcome sign.

We stand to begin our celebration.
We pray together,
"+In the name of the Father,
and of the Son,
and of the Holy Spirit."

The priest welcomes us by saying,
"The Lord be with you."

We answer,
"And also with you."

We praise and ask God to forgive us.

We pray:
"Lord, have mercy.
Christ, have mercy.
Lord, have mercy."

Draw yourself praying this prayer at Mass.

Glory to God in the highest,
    and peace to his people on earth.
Lord God, heavenly King,
almighty God and Father,
    we worship you, we give you thanks,
    we praise you for your glory.
Lord Jesus Christ, only Son of the Father,
Lord God, Lamb of God,
you take away the sin of the world:
    have mercy on us;
you are seated at the right hand
    of the Father:
    receive our prayer.
For you alone are the Holy One,
you alone are the Lord,
you alone are the Most High,
    Jesus Christ,
    with the Holy Spirit,
    in the glory of God the Father. Amen.

During the Mass we hear about God's love for us from the Bible. Sometimes we hear stories about how Jesus loved and cared for people.

After the first and second readings
we answer,
"Thanks be to God."

Before the gospel the priest or deacon
says,
"The Lord be with you."

We answer,
"And also with you."

The priest or deacon says,
"A reading from the holy gospel
according to _____ ."

We answer,
"Glory to you, Lord."

After the gospel reading we answer,
"Praise to you, Lord Jesus Christ."

After we listen to the readings and the homily, we pray the Creed together.

In this prayer we say we believe in God and in all things that Jesus teaches us through the Church.

Apostles' Creed

We believe in God, the Father almighty,
 creator of heaven and earth.
We believe in Jesus Christ, his only Son,
 our Lord.
 He was conceived by the power of the
  Holy Spirit and born of the
  Virgin Mary.
 He suffered under Pontius Pilate,
  was crucified, died, and was buried.
 He descended to the dead,
 On the third day he rose again.
 He ascended into heaven,
  and is seated at the right hand of
  the Father.
 He will come again to judge the living
  and the dead.
We believe in the Holy Spirit,
 the holy catholic Church,
 the communion of saints,
 the forgiveness of sins,
 the resurrection of the body,
 and the life everlasting. Amen.

Nicene Creed is on page 32.

Then we show we love others by praying for them.

Write a prayer for someone here.

God B Y for
them
I Love you
for d dot o

After each prayer, we answer,
"Lord, hear our prayer."

With the priest we thank God for the gifts we have to offer.

Then we answer,
"Blessed be God forever."

The priest begins the Eucharistic Prayer. During the prayer we pray:

Holy, holy, holy Lord, God of power
    and might;
heaven and earth are full of your glory.
    Hosanna in the highest.
Blessed is he who comes in the name
    of the Lord.
    Hosanna in the highest.

At Mass we remember the story of Jesus' Last Supper. The priest says and does what Jesus did.

The priest takes the bread and wine
and says the words of Jesus,
"Take this, all of you, and eat it;
this is My Body which will be given up
   for you."

"Take this, all of you, and drink
   from it;
this is the cup of My Blood,
the Blood of the new and
   everlasting covenant.
It will be shed for you and for all
so that sins may be forgiven.
Do this in memory of me.

We believe the bread and wine are now changed into Jesus Himself.

Decorate the banner.

The priest says,
"Let us proclaim the mystery of faith."

We answer,
"Christ has died,
Christ is risen,
Christ will come again."

Color the chalice.

The priest gives thanks to God for the gift of Jesus.

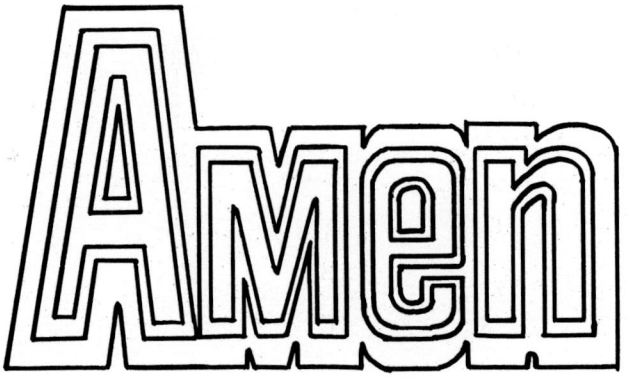

Decorate the word "Amen."

The priest says,
"Through him,
with him,
in him,
in the unity of the Holy Spirit,
all glory and honor is yours,
almighty Father,
forever and ever."

We answer,
"Amen."

At Mass we pray the prayer Jesus taught us. We pray the Our Father.

Draw Jesus teaching His friends to pray the Our Father.

Our Father

Together we pray,
"Our Father, who art in heaven,
hallowed be Thy name;
Thy kingdom come;
Thy will be done on earth
as it is in heaven.
Give us this day our daily bread;
and forgive us our trespasses
as we forgive those
who trespass against us;
and lead us not into temptation,
but deliver us from evil."

For the kingdom, the power,
and the glory are yours,
now and forever.

We share Jesus' gift of peace with one another.

The priest says,
"The peace of the Lord be with you always."

We answer,
"And also with you."

Draw yourself sharing the gift of peace with someone in your parish family.

With the priest, we pray for God's mercy.

Color the words we pray.

We pray,

"Lamb of God, you take away
 the sins of the world:
 have mercy on us.
Lamb of God, you take away
 the sins of the world:
 have mercy on us.
Lamb of God, you take away
 the sins of the world:
 grant us peace."

We prepare to receive Jesus in
Holy Communion.
We pray with the priest.

The priest says,
"This is the Lamb of God who takes
 away the sins of the world.
Happy are those who are called to
 his supper."

We answer,
"Lord, I am not worthy to receive
 you
  but only say the word
  and I shall be healed."

When we receive the host,
we hear the words,
"The Body of Christ."

We answer,
"Amen."

If we receive from the
cup, we hear the words,
"The Blood of Christ."

We answer,
"Amen."

Soon you will receive Jesus in Holy Communion.
What will you say to Jesus?

This is my prayer to Jesus.

At the end of Mass the priest asks God to bless our parish family.

Decorate the prayer.

The priest says,
"May almighty God bless you,
+ the Father and the Son,
and the Holy Spirit."

We answer,
"Amen."

The priest or deacon says,
"Go in peace to love and serve
the Lord."

We answer,
"Thanks be to God."

The Nicene Creed

We believe in one God,
  the Father, the Almighty,
  maker of heaven and earth,
  of all that is seen and unseen.

We believe in one Lord, Jesus Christ,
  the only Son of God,
  eternally begotten of the Father,
  God from God, Light from Light,
  true God from true God,
  begotten, not made, one in Being
    with the Father.
  Through him all things were made.
  For us men and for our salvation.
    he came down from heaven:
  by the power of the Holy Spirit
    he was born of the Virgin Mary,
    and became man.

For our sake he was crucified under
  Pontius Pilate;
  he suffered, died, and was buried.